POEMS
I COULDN'T SAY

LAKSHAY SINGH

notionpress.com

INDIA · SINGAPORE · MALAYSIA

for
the ones who
breathe rose dust

contents

contents

Welcome to sadness
The temperature is unbearable
Until you face it

– Lorde

battle cry

i usually tend to enjoy my own company
Rather be alone drowning overthinking
End of the day helps me sleep
Feels like that's what is best suited for me

Everything seems missing somehow
I accept the love I think I deserve
I loose the love I think I need
Realising I crave irony more than a mislead

There are pearls I regret for
At times I seek for a broken promise
I trust and fall very gently
Is grief ever the moral of the story?

I need balance
I feel betrayed
I hope for love
Is it the same ever?
There's nothing more I log for
More than an imperfect endeavour

Fatal emotions die within my bed
Never felt right, they always goodbye
I struggle and die a million times in my head
Rise from the dead
I heal
I deal
I die
I kneel

No love, its a battle cry
But there's a soul within me
Whispers to endure, rest's within me
Prays for logging we all desire
So I,
I breathe I breathe and I breathe

ache so deep and dearly

why does it weaken so much
Although I persuaded myself
Every-time I recall, how it escalated
It's so hurting forcing yourself
To loose the love for the one

Surreal accepted my fate
That I will have to hate you
Even it hurts so sweet and severely
I let go, I am tired of the misinterpretation
Even though it aches so deep and dearly

The souls hold the audacity
If you return happily, doors stay wide open
But they couldn't
Your face reflects the neglects I deed within
And they couldn't
Celebrate the empty arms
Turning away the sweet relief

I still wonder, but the smile changes at 2 am
Never wanted but couldn't escaped the way I loved you
I call for hell to you for what you made me sense
Brittle before I say,
I still feel for you but I wish you dead and dense

my man's a feeling

sitting at the lonesome chair
I feel like broken Ms. Blair
She comes up to me and ask's if I am okay
I said i am fine, just making away

Feeding on waves and bleeding bittersweet haze
I am trying to get well from the inside
As he still look's at me, glances into my folksy soul
But I won't feel the butterflies anymore

Wish I wasn't attached enough
Now it makes me cut right down
Beating stones and skipping tough
He always cries dripping salt and rough

She said we looked cute
Carries his fathers hair and praises the mother
This solitude was wrong about his emotion
Still chants and won't absorb the devotion

Remember at the second stair
Raised my eyebrows with pinched down breaths
There was emptiness on our faces
Like we did not sinked everyday at places

I lived for the serotonin
While he rugged my emotions, a bad phone in
Option, is that me?
Persuading that universe might have a plan
Stars called me a traitor, while I was still a young man

My mind is in a mirror maze

My heart is in some transactional phase

I want him but I don't want the poison again

And the precise long complain

The coffee inside me spills

I remember the rigid hands around my sore waist

As if it's crying altogether for the least

But as I blame it on life as much as I want

My man's a feeling

Makes me talk with ceilings

Makes me cry for healing

call it culture/call it folkways hey, want to hookup?

Remind me of innocence
So I can take time and scrutinise the moon forever
While it's crescents fall deeply into my eyes within
It doesn't remind me of anyone, it reminds me of innocence
My body my soul is in control, as if it's liberated

The folks surrounding my timeline are in deep despair
So was I, contained with lonesome pleasures
Forlornness is quite yet so loud
Ask my heart, how much I wish to escape

They name it culture or title the folkways
They all are broken, we all are sad until we aren't
While I was trapped within myself, within my solitude
I craved tenderness with the extremist souls
Forgetting what I actually wished for, kept on luring with the fouls

I wished love, I desired affection

But not with a consequence, not with choices

Wanted to feel seen and heard as if I was in a crowded room

After the hours felt guilty, as all of the strangers are wearing a costume

And I end up alone with my solitude, with my emptied contentment

The day the yearning blue moon had set, rises the ripening sun

Because I don't wanna be nothing, but free of the doomed strangers

Even if I don't deserve or earn the love we all look for

I will sit patiently free of solace but with a tranquil soul

A body infused with stability, a mind filled with maturity

kiss

I get lost in the alleys of my own thoughts
While I see you texting him, missing him
She caught me crying in a coffee shop
Waiting for the one who doesn't come

I am used to sit alone on a Thursday evening
Cracking the caffeinated wooden blocks
All of a sudden my soul shivers
It's nothing until it's everything to me

My hands ache to touch, to feel
Not just air and space but the essence of you
Not just rain and timber but the kiss of your lips
But when the night is over, you seem to not exist

one way or another (blame the universe)

It's so uneasy to make my truth be heard out of silence

My emotional system has always been complicated inside

My heart tries to find ones who can help to disarm it

I thought I can love you forever but your access seems like denial

The tables have turned as I saw them coming way before then

I had put my egoistic self at the very bottom to make you feel better

But I am so tired of this tip toeing, won't let history repeat itself

Can't be the fallen fruit in this story, so let me keep your belief off the shelf

My healers whispers to me to take a back step and save myself

Pain is bearable and I might miss you like I never did before

But my love for my frizzy papers is more than your denying love story

Never have I ever interfered in your lands but your balance is hallucinatory

Scared of separateness yet I blame myself for the wounds caused

One way or another you ended up being one of the hounds I wish to forget

This feels different than before because I don't feel sick or hurt

Maybe this is how the universe wanted it, I choose to escape before I fall for the dirt

not even twenty

When I breathe I feel the essence of nothing
I tend to survive on the verge of self talks lately
And I seem to be okay with it

It's a former routine of my ethereal self
I wake up, I try to nurture the best
And in the end I feel alone

Maybe a rose in the realms of despaired hounds
But if you ask my heart
The ones laughing are the deepest within

I don't wish to be like this anymore
But when accepted it's habitual
I am not even twenty and I am already tired

My potential is like a spreadsheet
The arrows are at peak and the mind is restless
I keep up the trial until its blown with thoughts

And then
I feel panicked, I feel guilty
I am not even twenty
And I am already so tired

eldritch

See how they are giggling at the marchers peak
While your faces and your thoughts decay like it's own moon crust's
Your body cries confined welcoming the evil

Look how you let the gates open
And I can sense their shivers of judgment over time
Your mind doesn't need to be weeping that loud
But no one hears you as there's silence all around

Tear drops ricochet, only the evil slurps
Serving the red crested drink
Fine crystal and sapphire doesn't make sense anymore
You shall bloom in your own time, don't kneel over the devils pharaoh

They might remark your guts and make you breathe eldritch
But you are your own, don't qualm your scarce blood
It's gifted from the unholy earthly mother
Exist the colloquialism of one's body
Generate the bonding of his own fondness
Your face reflects the scenic scars
It's halcyon
Forever ought it be

forsaken borders of thee mentalist

One must know how much I wish well
Crossing all the forsaken borders of thee empathy
Never have I ever regarded oneself a mentalist
Moon all over, I pity thee talk
Aye scarcely write the way I thought

Call myself overly demented for thee
Erstwhile being looney and holler
With maddening hunger and insanity
And I would write more about thee
Like tentacles into abysmal nothing

I wish I write the way aye forever wonder
Obsessively for thee, incessantly for thou
Manuscripts and pieces till I suffocate
Spiralling out like aye sorrowful empathy
Moments there are nothing left of aye legacy

I'd write aye self into nervous breakdowns

Whenever must know I wish well for thee

The verity is I do wish well and free

Aye sense wretched when I write the way I thought

Crossing all the forsaken border of thee fraught

she's the truth

Sitting across the still, embedded in the four walls
Contemplating with myself in the silence
Felt over neurotic so I teared up
My mother glanced and asked about the dilemma
While I felt nervy, I sighed no one cares
She said in a serene voice, no one cares

As I convince myself to go to bed
As I let my mind bully my heart
It feels so raw and inexplicable
This should not have lasted, but it's vast
It's hurting more than it should
My soul aspires to feel something at last

There's a concern, I told my mother
A flying dread of missing out on people
While every breath is falling in love around
Why do I tend to crave yet need to be left alone
My mother says to me, tell yourself it's fine
There's nothing greater than an individual's philosophical
mind

Possibly my enhance functions an another path
An exquisite way where my body rests
You might name it uncanny, the soil terms it blossoming
I feel so think-some, my thoughts are beautifully in galore
My mother speaks true, no one cares
But I do, the holy soul embedded asks caring
And surely I will, care and nurture with my whole

mislaid recital (smiling)

Mislaid in my mentation profoundly
While I roam freely in the tied up streets
I see people with a cause
Moving with all the loving acceleration

When I bump my shoulder incidentally
Wording a sorry is the last interaction
I smile with a cause
But it doesn't seem to do anything

It is gleeful to experience these everyday encounters
Yet so tiring for my self love interpretation
I love myself and pray for my body endlessly
But am I tired of this recital too?

It is wondering what a smile can do
Direct towards the "I don't care, I am okay"
But lie to you in a million ways
It is crazy how my smile can put silent
All of the hopeful expectations
And I end the day with " I don't care, I am okay"

visions of my home to my heart

It's been moments since the magic had been lost
But the visions and the stages never stop
I still hear the echoes that your sneakers make
Still find the stars a bit sunny
Still find the love constellations a bit funny

The ballets of my heart never stop racing
But I still haven't felt the worship
Do I even deserve you?
Or do you even deserve me?
What does free love even mean to me?

It's like I am perfumed with an obsession
An unlikely kind of personality I crashed into
We don't even talk about love enough
It's just a look in your eye, a ray of light on your collarbones
That calms me down that something's still not known

The walls whispers to me that there's still time
But I still haven't seen any spotlights on my empty stage
Take the microphone and sing a song to my heart
To anyone who might care, is it someone else? Is it you?
Just take my hand and save me from the due

I have never loved anyone
I have admired people and adored them enough
But where is the vision of my home to my heart
Is it about being patient ?
Is it about facing an adjacent ?
I still can't see it, I still don't feel it

the witches made of blood and gold

In between the leaping shadows of the wicked trees
I notice a glimpse of a man so tall with horns of blood
As I take my step forward with a thought so occurring
I am not scared of him, my love has been dragged enough through mud

He's a man with a motive, a man carrying the eyes of very old nick
Love is the game he gently asked me about
I went on my knees for his dear and failed to think about you
As I show my hands emptied and scarred, rest is what he might do

There I see him turning the page with shine of red and flesh
I might sign the book of the devil
Because I am so in love
And it hurts so much

I am better of as an enticing slave for the evil
Because loving someone, loving you is evil itself
So I accept the paper soaked in blood and sweat
And I sign the given for the evil himself

The doors open of my hidden seventh aura
He holds my hand and whispers his name within
I can see the witches made of blood and gold appearing
The soul takes it leave as I dance with devil tearing

the perks of my unilateral love

These eyes have been staying up all night
Talking to the one I fond
If you are a ghost please tell me
And if it's real make this heart discern

Loving you is like a laser quest
Makes me feeling like going home, curl up and die
You are the only one who makes me smile and cry
Makes me loose inside like fourth of July

you are the one I can't loose
you are the one makes me beat up inside
even if i tend to loose you some time
I will still wake up and root for you

I wonder how people will see us
when we will hold hands on the sidewalk
I will worship the ground we walk on
and I will worship the crossing we kiss on

I am faithful for long, fading away too soon
How do I tell you I love you?
How do I sing the perks I feel for you?
Every line I write says something about you

Sense me when you feel the need to
When that water pours it's love on my head
I don't blame it for crying and making sure I am okay
Because every time I cry, I sing what you said
Because every time I sigh, I relive your touch in my bed

to, anyone who might care

Its alright
To wave at your reflection in your own tears
Sometimes
Inhale and exhale doesn't work out
Just passed by
As no one cares about your willing lullaby

Its alright
To realise how cruel and unfair this world can get
Sometimes
Take a step, then take a step back
Just passed by
Felt so lonely I'd rather choose to die

Its okay
To not keep stands with the strange appearing hounds
Sometimes
Read a book from my therapist
Just passed by
Are you acting like my serial monogamist?

Its unfair

How decent and carefree you look

Sometimes

Hold my hand or just chant the love series

Just passed by

So ignorant, with your misunderstood theories

Its not okay anymore

I can just leave if I want to

Sometimes

But the cries stops me

Just passed by

Maybe for real this time

broken realms

Usually end up so solicit
Erstwhile termed as the stoic one
I am so tired of myself being this significant
Solitude and emptiness
Is awfully comforting now

Willingly stay through the noon of night
I am aware this is not the end, yet its degrading
Confide, rely, belief
Brings out the best in self
I desire to figure out these broken realms

It's just that
Your selfless apprise won't help me
Isolation in my comfort book might be
The only eluding kind
It is my favourite time

A gracious mind filled with opinions
Craving for stillness, slowness and care
Assure you that no soul no man would mind
It is the greatest
Wandering with them without them feels the same

There has been exertion of none
Couldn't even feel the intension
Why would I?
When there has been not even one
Stuck in the art of being alone

Avoidance from the hypocrites can be
The only escapist dime
My earnest hands won't mind
Rallying with the lonesomes
Earning the littlest of being myself
It allows reflection, I fall deeper
It's a blessing yet a curse
Observant, mindful, sensitive
It's solace

voicemail

Peculiar of me searching for comfort over chaos
While you exit my turbulent psyche
I still wish you were resting behind me
Moved on happily a while ago
But you were my one devotion

Practiced meditation to blank out your touch
Buried the frames so I could sigh out loud
Left the city to get me going
I realised you don't deserve me
But I can't nigh my selflessness

Wish you well like never did before
Standing at the corner with my false heroism
But I breathe in the voicemails left behind
You left the roof over my distorted head
But I still stand at the edge
Think about us
With a broken thread

god damn bracelet

I sneak you in my fragile heartfelt apartment you dreamt about

My eyes are full of sparkle when i see you get comfortable in my bed

I feel so struck by moonlight when you touch the paintings in my room

god forgive this poor heart of mine, how I was so much in love with you

I don't know why I still have kept the left alone bracelet which deserves so much more

I wonder where is the one I gave you, is it in the gutter or kept safely in your closet

Is it even possible to fall this deeply and feel this within overnight

god help me forget what it felt like to be never be spoken about again

I wish I had never let my hopeless foot on the door when your text chimed

I hate myself for saying this that your arms felt like home to me more than home

But i promise that I will never hurt someone like you do

God tell me how to get over my silly talks floating in my brain

Don't you worry about anything

The bracelet is kept safely but it has accepted it's faith

It doesn't reflect your hurt but radiates what my care for you was

I live this life without a lifesaver

I feel deeply the not survivable

But dear god i know you are counting down my tears at 3 am

I put my head down to you that I will be stronger and still alluring

the kiss, the smoke, the conversation, the god damn bracelet

I forgive it all

But dear god pardon my words

I will never forget what I felt

I will never forget how heavy was my chest

Hope I feel alright as nothing ever rests

solar eclipse/loosen ends

Too unalterable until my spirit breaks down by itself
You know you too important
You know you too invisible to my probing eyes
You know how much I rely on your endeavouring

But what if I do that no one ever expected
What if I let you loose, will I ever?
What if I leave without a justification
What if I leave without a letter with my name on it

What form will my cruelty take
While the crusty wind I gasp on
What ends will I keep loose and tighten
While the solar eclipse changes into the lunar one

explain myself later?

My feelings are hurt but I am pretending they're not
I am overly consumed in my confinement but I don't sigh
It's so lonely sometimes but I still make through the day
I tend to feel like I am gonna live forever when I know I am not
My emotiveness is exhausted, can I explain myself later?

I still do elucidate, here comes the river of my flamed sentiments
When the sunshine hides it's hope, I loose it all again
It's not that I don't admire observing world pass by while I sit at the edge
But when my coffee is over, why do I miss the people who have I never met
I can feel my overshared anxiety kicking in, can I explain myself later?

This is not me expounding, it's him that has been fooled by desolation

A million times I walk around thinking how will I end today

Will it be the sickness of feeling alone again or will the over caffeinated heart sum it up

Will it be the nothing new conversations or will I blame it on time and tend to sustain

I have been down this alley before, can I explain what I am feeling later?

But the time is through and I wear poetry like a dress with roses full of decency

I wish to put a stop on my oversharing but I am not used to people holding my hand

Don't want my inner self to recall the feeling and let my hands do the writing

I love being alone , I wish to observe , I want to stay silent

But when it rains heavily and my hands aren't warm enough

I want a friend, I wish to kiss my lover, I want my time turn into emotions

There's a saying by the cleansed beings that everything will be alright, it's just about time

And I very well know myself that blaming the clock calms me down

But I have been roaming, my steps don't stop searching for a real attachment

To the one I can let my shoulder on and don't hesitate sharing my caffeine

Forgive me, I think I am over disclosing

I will be okay, can I explain myself later?

living lost disaster (ft. her)

met this boy
he's a living lost disaster
loved him still, thought I could fix it
but god what a fucking looser master

Saw him only as my loving friend
until he asked me to kiss him
okay it's fine, but then he did it
like every other little boy i quit

His vibration ain't that bad
i liked what was done and said
but baby if i write a poem about you
That means i am actually really hurt

Now i tell everyone the moments won
While i turn the lost and found into blanked words
So the whole world can know how foolish you are
Keep that to yourself, shut up and au revoir

No one's breaking my heart and soul
And you don't deserve to be satisfied by my cherry heart
I still wear that bracelet, Karma saw it first
I will let you cry about it

french scream

Is it wrong to wait for the near end of you
Overthinking the ways I do
Sinner psychotic body of mine, you call it
I wish you loved me more calmly, you couldn't

I only listen to this, your waving notes of nervousness
All because I asked you to explain why you did
You say you are just neighbours within the block
But do the neighbours know when do you feel loved

You think I am dumb and stupid, because I am in love
No way I don't feel the way you do, I loved you more
And here you come screaming at me for asking why I did
If you really wish to open your mouth, scream to me in French

At last I saw your face black and white as it was the truth
I was near the aisle thinking and crying, you couldn't explain
All of the worries about you were so true and blue
I hope when you scream again, he finds it french and new

the victimising kisser

I had my eyes on you vividly
You kept your hands up my waist
I felt pretty yet so misused
Obviously it went away with a deep sigh
But I didn't see the warning of you acting victimised

My intensity towards your noisy hair was a love language
Seemed like your only intention was to touch the night
I feel in love with you but I fell out of it sooner
Kind of delighted that my surrounding is cleaner and deepen
You won't be affecting my glory, it has already had enough

The sixth sense of my conscience won't even count you as a lesson
You were just an experience, one who is lost in his own cause
Why was I expecting adore from you?
You are just a boy, nothing well knit man about you
Those who can't love themselves can't cherish the angels surround

Lovingly and tenderly I wish you spend favourable days

I consider myself an individual with wings and gratitude

Not the one to put you down, make you cry for longitivtiy

But as you put yourself beneath the earth to make feel falseness

As you roam around like a parasite with a joint between your teeth

As you make try to hurt the angels surround with your non actuality

Unworthy of my beautiful and gentle kiss, I wish it reminds you of how karma tastes

I wish it stays on your collar forever until you love yourself how I do to myself

the hopeful yearns of your seraphic touch

I have been leaping beneath the padded shores
I have been out-breathing my inner soul
Running out of misery, I feel it off my shoulder
Love is so diaphanous to me

There isn't a shortage overwhelmed
I sense and perceive it all around me
From those high kneel proposals
To the candle witch hazel kisses

Like a devoid inside of me, a dream
I crave the whispers and the seraphic touch
A not so broken angel I remind myself
There's still time
There's still a flare of the hopeful burn

Not yet healed or ready
Should I be going to steady
Just want to know is this love completely off the table?
If I let you in, can you prove it to me?
Because I need you to calm me down babe

– Ariana grande

strange to be in love with a stranger

Met you once and I felt loved a thousand times

How do you perceive to do this? I don't even know what's your job yet

You seem to know how to touch my hand beautifully

I just lent you my keys to drive for the evening

And turns out you know the roads to my heart already

The way you speak with your words dancing towards me

It's like a tune of folk I know since childhood

We were supposed to call out names and practice goodbyes

How am I supposed to? My heart sense's prosperity and at ease

You are just a stranger and it's strange to be in love with a stranger

I heard how you wished to stay too while our cheeks made love

You didn't talk as much as you wished to, you watched me speak millions

Your little profound laughs to your side edged eyebrows, I miss them

Now I am back home at last writing about your crusted lips of sun

You very well know how to kiss mine, I miss them

Tonight I kissed a stranger

After hours I fell in love with a stranger

Strange to be in love with a stranger

But I did and this love doesn't feel strange at all

scarlet blush

Call it a prodigy
While I am tuning up with teakwood flames
God has it's own ways, rather accidental
Yet it feel so loveable and gentle
An impact so scarlet and maroon
Making me dive, deep down into the moon

Make it a fantasy
A story so undreamed of
Says who that threatened doesn't love
Or a scarred won't get any above
All it took was a gifted touch
I have never felt this beloved, it's too much

Keep on chanting, they mention it till death
That I deserve the love
I can preserve the love
But as the path's too good to be true
Worthwhile as it feels not true at all, a dream
I open and see you, runs the love in my bloodstream

Hush the the speeches
I can still feel the evenings coffee of your lips
The bittersweet loving I deserve, god gifted indeed
Without bleeding the moonlight agreed
Tender hints you spill all over my body
That I am being loved like the tales
Proves the evermore scarlet blush on my face

our band

While I was going to label it as a random evening and go to
bed

It's suppose to be midnight and I am used to close my eyes

But when I open after a breath, it's the best night ever

You made me realise that manifestation is not a joke

And I am not kidding when I say you remind me of cigarettes
after sex

I would ditch every plan out of the window to be in your
arms instead

K, apocalypse, sunsets, heavenly, affection, sweet and cry

My heart refuses to recite if it's not about you

I call them "our band" as if they were made to sing about us

You made me realise that smoking cigarettes is different

Different when it hits you all around and you are deeply in love

And if mine is over, you kiss me to remind me the taste of it

I might have been falling in love and scared of it

But if its about running my hands through your dry hair

If its about laughing and giggling while you try to kiss me

If its about sitting on your lap and feeling the warmth of your hands

If its about a goodbye kiss and exchanging bracelets

I am not scared of it at all

stay out of my papers

For once
as i move the rusted perfect pencil of mine
start with crying and end up with a smile
i am done with an another piece of art

I call
I call myself a latching artist hungry for lines
Weather it is love or fear, i hate it now
My desire to write is struck by the glue

Please now
I met you i saw you i love you, I don't wish to jot down
The moon calls me out to write about you
But for once
Stay out of my papers and lay down in my arms

write me your song

The vivid warmth of the hands I cherish
Falls the moonshine every evening
I fall in love and I pray to fall even deeply
It's the vocalist of my bed clock, I fall asleep to the tune

My heart is hopelessly slowed and loved
While your undressed words are around my neckline
I want you to write me your song, filled with affinity
So I can sing to my mother how much you love me

It is your morning articulation or the moonlight emphasise
Ever since you touched me the way you do
The lovingly soulfulness of my favoured body
Your overflowing heart seems to claim it out of thin air

My passion is you and my admiration is how my face fits perfectly on your chest

While it rests so tenderly, I can feel your heart pumping the song you wrote

Your blood seems to leave your control and run through my fallen veins

I fall deeply and ever more as each moment pass by

And it seems like my laid down love for you will keep falling deeper, deeply within

silly conversations

Stepped off the usual day and you came along

I don't even know your name yet and I think I know you since forever

My face is red and confused as you don't stop smiling

We can't be romantics but I miss the way you were ticklish

I miss the way my heart was allured and rising

You wish to fall deeply within my heart, I see it in your true eyes

There is no hiding in speaking the truth that you made me feel easier

Easier to love and breezier to kiss, while my hands rest on yours

Bless my heart how I miss your giggling over me calling you silly

And now here I am at 4 am writing about our silly conversations

I wish we could be more and forever then some

But we both know the sides of our stories

As you leave me smiling with open doors never to be closed

I will miss the sundown on your chin when I go away

I hope we crash in another lifetime, to be around kissing and supposed

real love baby

As the sun takes upon it's strike there's a vitality
My heart which I wear outside my body for you to love
It starts pouring out it's moonlight without my decision
Baby let me dance to the notes, you are my musician

I feel super lofted like I am on the clouds hovering
Probably because when I see you in my dreams I redden
This body of mine won't stay free in my bed at home
Can I crash at your place? I demand your lips while I finish
this poem

The truth shall be told that you went first but I fall harder
every day
When that golden body of yours touches my vivid shivers
I feel the sensation of what it must be like for god to love
No kind creature in love on this land is unworthy of

You smell like my favourite wine from the 90's
The way you crack eggs reminds me of my mother
I love it when you feed the cats, reminds me of my father
Whenever I look in your hazel eyes, feels like real love baby

what did Krishna do?

There's beauty everywhere, you just need to seek for Krishna in it

As Krishna is beauty and so is you

Feels like you are some sort of his beloved roop (form)

I saw the beauty you talked about, oh Krishna what did you do?

I don't wish to talk about the blunt expectations

Because there were none wanted

One call in this modern backyard

Made the upcoming events unforgettably beautiful

Seems more like a plan by almighty when you arrived

Didn't knew it would be this hard to let you go

I blame Krishna for his games that he made us play

Indeed made me realise what true love might be

How much I adore and pray my gratefulness for what he did

And how much I fond and miss the Krishna I saw in your heart

I wont ever let go the letter you left and the flowery scent you put

You will always be in my heart forever and the way you looked

The comfort of your tall shoulder and the breeze in your eyes

I am still thinking about the Krishna in you, left me mesmerised

As Krishna is beauty and so is you

Feels like you are some sort of his beloved roop (form)

I saw the beauty you talked about, oh Krishna what did you do?

it's a yes (ft. him)

What did Krishna do ?
You Asked
Here's the answer you must claim

Was looking for eroticism
but love came to me unexpectedly
you became the happiness key all around
when i met you i was a little scared and afraid what might do
but thank God i dared my intention
I got lost in your sweetness
Your smile's deepness
Sitting with you was the best of it all
Made me forgot the life's tearing test
Three days felt like years like I have been longing for this
forever
i never thought this would make me admire and in tears

तुम बारिश की बूंदे हो
तुम कृष्ण की मुरली हो
तुम सपना थे जो अब साकार हो
तुम लक्ष्य थे पर अब तुम मेरा प्यार हो

i feel tasteless, you fix that

Don't want or need it on the cell, this ain't it
Stop testing my patience with these walls
I might flick up my existence for your moisture
I don't need no other night with myself

Brush your taste on my shiny tongue while I feel tasteless
You know how to fix it very well, you make your move
I am a killer while I get to see your affect on my features
Keep your look on my breath, turn my hair into stardust

Shivers down my thighs or is it my downtown heart
I just want to be heard and whisper your name
Out of breath but I feel the unbeatable flame
Staying out of the lane would be ridiculous, you deserve more and more

Praying for your touch to Jesus will be sin, call me out as your sinner

My body defy's gravity when I reach out for your trace on my borderline

There are secrets I wanna spill, stories I want to claim

You make me forget about every of my unfinished business

You will turn every breath of mine to evil, that's just a myth

Even if your mystical blood makes me a crime, my mouth awaits

And forever it will do so be thirsty for it

dived in blue ink

I don't know about you or your patterns yet
Have i met your bodied presence, not yet
but when you lay down your words on me
It's my love language you seem to speak

So soft and fluent with my heart
And when you are asleep in blue
My heart whistles it's adore thinking about you
And in the morning there's a calmness within I wake up with

I haven't even touched you but I can feel your skin on my fingertips
Wandering and ruining my sleep cycle I take care of gently
My aura's exhausted and my body asks me back to sleep
But if it's you, I will smother it once and twice and then thrice

all you can do is be here with me whenever you can
I know you can't yet but i will wait for the while
Scared that I might get latched on and make you leave
Messy and overwhelming but i can love you

While i hide it all being dressed in serene
Hold my hand with your dived in blue ink palm
This is more than i can think of for the beginning, i am sorry
this is me for you
Imperfect and incomplete

You might do think about what i am afraid of
I do too, a lot indeed
Whatever you saw and touched before with your softly clues
I have been stuck by you and loving you as if i am hurting
you

I do and I want to
love you

i never knew
This could be you
I never knew
This could be me

scent of my pillows

Yes I see the affection your eyes reflect while you are at the airport

I am here in my bed staring at my phone hoping I could be with you

Even the words are decreasingly few for my brain to describe

What my mystical heart which rests with you goes through

When I dream about you, when I think about you

It's not fair but acceptable that you are a thousand miles away

Nothing really matters to me, I can catch a flight now or run on the runway

But for the moment I keep my hand on my heart and breathe for a second

I perfume myself with your love and smile after you check in

Now I sleep with your calm scent on my pillows

Dream like of me how I add you in my daily prayers

I can wait for days that will be longer or years to be shorter

I will wait for your whimsical touch

I will wait for your calming essence

I will wait to kiss you again softly on your wondrous cheek

I can wait for you and I surely will

Even if it takes infinity or a thousand weeks

dear lover, I miss your salty hands

He doesn't think twice when my name seems to be around

The first train in the morning he boards

So I can put my head on his homelike shoulder

Whatever he says doesn't feel actual

My soul seeks for the sunshine he provides, it's like supernatural

The moment he got off that train, my body turned down rivers

I could sense the warmth of his rigid salty hands from miles away

Staring at the ceilings waiting for the announcement to be made

And then there he comes running towards me with his bouquet

Might not be the same green lands we breath on, but in my heart he's here to stay

It's so silly of me

How I take every little moment as a sign from the universe

But how can I deny the white butterfly that sat on my forehead

While I pray for it to rain and the next day it pours romantically

Something about you, something about us is insanity

As I lock tight the moments we had spent and cherish on

I thank god for whatever he had planned for our little life

The names we had exchanged, to the loving Oliver from the deary Elio

It hurts how I will rely on your beloved scent you left behind

My body and soul will wait for you until our love is redesigned

The devils make me see around differently
Look what are they doing, crawling under my skin
I think about my inner wealth, my self hood
As they keep flipping the revealed sentiment of
my angelic soul
I sit here beside the shining sun with a rose quartz
Smiling at the stars healing
I am just a boy, I am just so young, I am just so grateful
Breathing and just tuning

– Lakshay singh

power of the heavenly sphere

Six bodied surrounded
I am not alone
Levitating on this hash ground of evils
It takes time to be yourself

While the snow falls
I bided with my mindfulness
As the evil had spread
I piled up, rose from the dead

They asked me to leave
They made me teary till I bleed
But it didn't cry all after
Made the most of it, went quite

Eyes filled with meditated
Hands around myself protected
The aura speak's for itself
I transformed in my presence

They wont enter the orbit
My power encircles it
I feel unchangeable than ever
It will keep me soul, it will keep me protected
Will fail the need for endeavour

adams ale

Ethereal of my spirit, when she calls for supper
Hideout in the vacant rainfall on my skin
My body doesn't ask to step on the pedestal I was born
I can't make it all the way home
Let my sinking be in the herb fields, which I used to roam

It levitates and makes me the loftiest
How much I pray to leave you all behind
And match my fragile silky hair to the core
Let my inner selfhood wave with the Adams ale

The crescent moon and the dipped in blue mother
Smiled at me, gazed with felicity
While I was howling along with the soughing leaves
Grounding with the trees and playing cranberry
Fleeing as a toucan with it's Jesus verse
How much I ask to run away in the greenwoods
Quitting them behind, where they can't find me to knead

lately 1

It's golden to witness lately

Getting more and more absorbent with my ocean

Letting in all the unfamiliar feelings to deepen my surroundings

I am only 16

But,

Lately loving being divergent and pouring flaked caffeine

It was hard to understand, hard to get casual with

A youthful sinked mind just wandering with the tides

A broken summer heart just hovering above the glides

I am not sentimental

But,

Lately realising how time says goodbye for a change

Never really believed the cry can gain self control

There was bad and there might be worse

Some sort of negative magnetic pole

But,

Lately picking up the tears cried, watering the optimistic greens

The inner vision and the mystical ambition
Always arise a soul to be expressed yet
Growing second by second and then all at once
But,
Lately I have been leaving
Lately I have been feeling
Lately I have been dealing
Lately I have been easing

lately 2

I have been travelling and crossing boundaries without any company lately.

Exploring, existing and breathing locals without any external tension.

The co vertigo's, I am realising every second I breathe that it's okay to be alone and sigh.

I did had some panic attacks because of my dreaded loneliness but with euphoric calming wind around me it went away too.

i have been taking situations slowly recently

feeling awful some hours down but Matt Haig wipes off my tears

lately I am living and self giving

It's pretty well and fine

I will be okay like the last times

equinox

As far as is it seems, it's closer than I hoped for it to be

This beautiful sighting alluding right in front of my eyes

But how do you anticipate on my belief that I see the light

It's scorching beam is journeying through my avoiding skin

I want to hit that light but my concealed offering controls me

The sorrowed thinker deep inside me wants to communicate

While my feet spreads out towards the sun rays

My fingertips ache wiping the doubted soul of my selfhood

The dandelions can heal me while I let my breath sync with
the autumn

I let my mindfulness born with a heave towards the rising
moonlight

My divine intellect regards to be so rooted with the wooden flesh

That the absence or the silly presence of any defect won't affect me

Where's the spirituality of the wandering conifers , accept me in your conscience

I can't let my exile be in the arms of the bitter, let me spread along with you

Let me pick up the lemongrass and taste the berries of your forgiven love

If my body ever resides, let it be in the waves of the airing sunlight

Don't let my delightful soul and mind to let serve the greedy ones

I don't want my emotions and feelings which are so deep within

Be rusted around the dark nowhere, dedicate it to the power of sunburn

The love it shines upon without the verdicts, I let myself breathe with the creator

it's a beautiful world
(at last)

I want this show to fade away slightly

Want the table so remorse turn upside down

Without the caved in ending I wish the end of this world

I don't really care what it takes, I seek change and a radical burn

My mind at up-stake want you to loose the loosened

You deserve so much more, the soul you rest with prays for you

There is no body without the idea of giving up on love and trust

Surely you can assure yourself with affinity, build your empire of gold dust

You should feel like a hovering bird with blue wings

When you see yourself in the mirror, you better feel alright

And when you stop chasing the flood of the sick and sad

We eternally rise as we take our time to be

As the sun shines and you let the moonlight glimpse upon you
We stand and endure while we end our lies
And sort out who we really are
We make our body humbled by breaking down the pattern

We walk down the path waiting, we grow and we flourish
Like the flowers in your garden
Like the falcon in the sky
Like the newly born fish in the pond
We make ourselves surround with angel dust, as we are too be
The angels of this beautiful world, we are meant to be

healers in power
(i take you with me)

My eyes ache when I look around, there's got to be so much more

Everyday and everyone around my surroundings which I tend to gate keep

Felt awful, vulnerable, innocent yet so submerged deeply

If I ever find the path to step out of this loop, I take you with me

Definitely there's got to be more

How can I not deny that the ones walking are full of sorrow and seek freedom

I am one of you while I define my presence with words that bleed dry

My soul strives for serenity, likewise my brain seeks stability

If I ever step out of this flaming room, I take you with me

Definitely there's got to be something more

As the time takes it cause and just like magic we tend to evolve

Just take a deep breath your body reflects, let those feet hit the waters

We aren't afraid of the difficult hounds, our healers are in power now

Take my hope of cries while I step out with my angels

There's a path to this, let me guide you

Look here we are barefoot far away from the unseasoned places

Now count your steps and pick up your carnelian stone as it holds you

Can you hear the unrealistic voice of the ocean as it speaks, can you feel the energy

Breathe out as we touch the infinity together to make the auras realise

There much more of the sun rays illuminating awaiting to heal

There's no wrong decision to be made, this is where your soul rests to be

Every face enhances a new emotion, every ray as it hits develops a new expression

Let the over surfaced mind of yours drift away with the winds you diffuse with

Step into the quite realm of harmony with us

There's much more evolving and healing to be absorbed, you are worthy of it

all because of you, all because of me
(the end, thank you)

Tinted exhausted blush on my cheeks
Seems to be taking place in my skin as the candle fades
I was all by myself throughout this process I name
When I let what crawled through under, to let go

It has been waiting for two years now
I really hate to admit the time and pride it took
How young, loved and stupid I must have felt
That I ended up with a story to tell of my own

Won't lie I feel grateful sometimes to go through all
Because look at me now, here I sit with a rose quartz smiling
Under the moonlight I manifest the best of me
Rather it be some love story, rather it be some confusing
glory

I guess I still might cry myself to sleep
And pick them up because it is a never ending loop
But on the other side I don't have to be
I just think, feel, experience, love, cry, move, shine
Sometimes dance, sing, swim, try, align

This is me all because of you
This is me all because of me
Forever it will be
My happy sad confused ending
And I love it

author bio

Lakshay Singh, eighteen, is a medical student and an author of two poetry collections published earlier. He took a gap year after graduating from high school to figure out what he wishes to pursue in the future. He ventured into poetry and writing at the age of fifteen. It started as a form of interest, he posted his poetry on social media and as his interest grew he decided to publish a collection of his own writings.

His debut book 'Midnight ecstasy, Midnight Sorrow' then his sophomore book titled 'Unknown lullabies'.

Singh loves to write about the complicated classic love and different situations in life that one goes through and can relate to. His speciality is to focus on various human emotions felt by someone and turn them into classic poetry for the readers to relate.

Poems I Couldn't Say' is Singh's third official poetry collection. The idea for this book came when he started thinking about how every human is so different and unique from each other and their emotions too. How a person can feel and absorb an emotion in several ways which a human mind can't comprehend but the heart can. He wrote these poems during his last year of school and during his gap year.

www.ingramcontent.com/pod-product-compliance
Lightning Source LLC
Chambersburg PA
CBHW031438130726
47989CB00003B/1200